HOMEMADE

▲ ▲ ▲ ▲ ▲

ORGANIC SKIN
& BODY CARE

'A conscious approach to health & wellness'

carmabooks.com

*You are invited to to join our **Free Book Club** mailing list. Sign up via our website to receive **special offers** and **free for a limited time** Health & Wellness eBooks!*

HOMEMADE

▲▲▲▲▲▲

ORGANIC SKIN & BODY CARE

Easy **DIY RECIPES** & Natural
Beauty Tips for Glowing Skin

Carmen Reeves

Disclaimer

This book provides general information, experiences and extensive research regarding health and related subjects. The information provided in this book, and in any linked materials, are not intended to be construed as medical advice. There are no 'typical' results from the information provided - as individuals differ, the results will differ. If the reader or any other person has a medical concern, he or she should consult with an appropriately licensed physician or health care worker. Never disregard professional medical advice or delay in seeking it because of something you have read in this book or in any linked materials.

Carma Books
carmabooks.com

hello@carmabooks.com

CONTENTS

INTRODUCTION

CHAPTER 1

A Natural Approach to Radiant Skin

CHAPTER 2
Softening and Beautifying Your Skin

CHAPTER 3
Indulge Your Body with Natural Bath Products

CHAPTER 4
Nutritive DIY Formulas for Nails, Hair and Skin Restoration

CHAPTER 5
Making a Dazzling Impression

CHAPTER 6
Therapeutic Facial Care

Cleansers, Toners and Intensive Treatments for that Beautiful Face **63**

*For more recipes to achieve beautiful,
shiny hair, you may benefit from my book:*
**Homemade Natural Hair Care
(with Essential Oils)**

INTRODUCTION

The Truth about Commercial Beauty

We all want to look and feel our best, but at what price are we paying for our pursuit of beauty? There are hundreds of thousands of commercial body care products out there; from creams, lotions and body scrubs to make-up and deodorant, all available in your supermarket, online and even in natural food markets. Most of them claim to soften our skin, improve our appearance or make us smell great, but the majority of these products contain toxic chemicals, synthetic preservatives, artificial fragrances, colors and mineral oils which are all too often animal-tested before making it to the shelf.

Many of us use an average of over 10 body care products daily, bombarding our bodies with hundreds of different chemicals each day. Over 10,000 ingredients can be used to make these products, including harsh substances like formaldehyde, carcinogens, parabens, plus a cocktail of other synthetic ingredients and toxins. While many of these elements can be irritating to the skin itself, they can also be absorbed into our bloodstream causing sensitivities and potential long-term health risks. The skin is our largest organ, after all, so we need to be aware that what we apply on our skin can and will end up inside our bodies.

Ninety percent of personal care products contain Sodium Lauryl Sulfate (SLS). This is a known skin, lung and eye irritant that interacts and combines with other chemicals to form nitrosamines—which are mostly carcinogenic. Parabens, also found in personal care products such as deodorants, shampoos, make-up and lotions, contain estrogen-mimicking properties that have been linked to breast cancer *(Byford, 2002; Pugazhendhi, 2007)*. And the list goes on.

You Can Stop the Toxic Cycle

Fortunately, there is a way to look radiant and beautiful while still having the peace of mind knowing that you are not damaging your skin and compromising your health each day. With a little help from nature, you can take your health into your own hands while consciously caring for your beautiful body, the animals and the environment. This plant-based body care system not only ensures that no animals were harmed in product testing or manufacturing, it also means that no toxic substances are going onto your skin and into your body. By simply using organic body care ingredients, you are taking a big step toward a healthier and more sustainable lifestyle.

Throughout this book, *Homemade Organic Skin & Body Care,* I will empower you to treat yourself to a youthful, radiant glow from the inside out, using the nutritive and organic ingredients that your skin deserves. Featuring all-natural ingredients such as flowers, oil blends and fresh fruits, I have researched and formulated these replenishing recipes to prove to you that harmful, synthetic chemicals are not necessary to enjoy a glowing, healthy look and feel. You can create these recipes in your own home with simple ingredients and equipment from your kitchen, garden or pantry.

The Benefits of Homemade Organic Skin & Body Care

Firstly, I'd like to share something with you. For a long time I was suffering from low energy levels, high allergen levels and felt as though my mind was in a constant fog. Not finding the answers to my many questions about why I was feeling this way through traditional means or prescribed antidotes, I began researching the effects of natural and organic ingredients on a person's physical and mental well-being. By simply cutting the amount of toxins I put in and on my body, I noticed an increase in my energy levels, my allergies were alleviated plus my mind (and my skin!) were clear.

Your Skin Will Thank You

The benefits of using homemade organic body care can be felt and seen upon immediate use. Once you start making and using your own all-natural creations, you'll never look back to using commercial alternatives. The healing properties of homemade organic body care far outweigh those of their commercial and synthetic counterparts. They are anti-inflammatory, stimulating and soothing to the skin. Plus, they are loaded with anti-aging properties including antioxidants and vitamins to help achieve a youthful glow.

Cocoa butter adds calming relief for eczema and psoriasis, whereas commercial creams and lotions can be loaded with irritants. Many toxins in store-bought items will clog your pores inhibiting healthy skin; in contrast, diluted tangerine juice, with its antibacterial and antifungal properties, is a great ingredient for healthy pores without the risk of side effects. Preservatives in commercial body care products are sometimes the most toxic components. So, why put parabens and coal tar dyes on your body when natural Vitamin E Oil, with its antioxidant properties, can act as a preservative in your butters and lotions?

Other lifestyle choices can have an impact on your skin's health in conjunction with these organic body care recipes. For instance, it has been shown that a diet rich in plant-based foods (a colorful rainbow of fruits and vegetables), ample exercise, plenty of water and a reduction in your exposure to environmental pollutants (such as smoking) can positively contribute to your radiant glow.

It's Easy, Sustainable and Cost-Effective

Making your own organic body care products is not only healthy but practical. It's an affordable way to enjoy a luxurious skin care system, designed just for you, without spending money on expensive brands. Plus, you will always know exactly what ingredients are in your body care products and from where they were sourced.

Many of the ingredients used in making your own body care products will already be in your pantry while others can be purchased, often in bulk, at natural food markets or online. Depending on product availability and your personal budget, opt for ingredients labeled 'organic' whenever possible. By choosing organic, fewer toxins will be applied to your skin, and you will be supporting sustainable cultivation while helping the environment by lessening the impact of the chemical manufacturing industry.

It's Time to Experience a Healthy Glow

So when you walk down the aisle in the supermarket and look at the hundreds of body care products with additives like Sodium Lauryl Sulfate and Isopropyl Alcohol, you will be armed with the comfort and knowledge of having your own nutritive, gentle, all-natural products, that you created yourself, at home.

Are you ready to ditch those chemicals and embrace your inner eco-chic beauty? I am sure you will love the benefits of these easy-to-follow organic body care recipes that will nourish your skin and invigorate your senses. After trying and testing the various formulas in this book, it's my aim to help you detoxify your body using effective, proven remedies and my hope is that you will find your own favorites among the recipes and tips—to enjoy for a lifetime. A healthy glow has never felt so beautiful.

Before You Begin

These recipes are formulated to be kind and gentle to your skin, but if you have any sensitivities or are concerned about any ingredients, a patch test is a quick and easy way to find out if your skin will react to a certain substance.

Try a Patch Test

Simply apply a small amount of the ingredient in question onto the center of a Band-Aid *(see dilution guide for essential oils below).* Then place it on the inside of your forearm. Leave it there for 24 hours. If the area becomes irritated before that time is up, take the Band-Aid off and rinse gently with cold water making sure not to scrub, as that may cause further discomfort. If the reaction does not subside seek help from a healthcare practitioner. After 24 hours, remove the Band-Aid and look for signs of redness, swelling or other irritation. If the skin looks normal, the ingredient should be safe to use. If you find yourself sensitive, you can personalize the recipe by replacing the ingredient with another natural alternative.

Using Essential Oils

Essential oils are highly concentrated and extracted from the leaves and roots of various plants, with various therapeutic, aromatic and cosmetic uses. Due to their high potency and concentration, it is important to use them correctly and sparingly. Avoid the use of undiluted or highly concentrated essential oils directly on the skin unless indicated; lavender is one of the few essential oils that can be used 'neat', or directly on the skin undiluted, a drop or two at a time. If performing a patch test, ensure to dilute as per the chosen recipe. As a general rule, 1 drop of essential oil should be diluted with 5ml of carrier oil before being applied to the skin. Do not ingest essential oils and keep out of reach of children and pets. Ensure essential oils do not come into contact with your eyes and use with caution if you are pregnant, planning to become pregnant or have any pre-existing medical conditions.

Diluting with Carrier Oils

Carrier oils are vegetable-derived oils that can be used in your body care recipes as a base or to dilute essential oils before being applied on the skin. These oils can be alternated, combined, or used in place of one another depending on availability, therapeutic or textural preference, or skin sensitivities. Some people may find themselves sensitive to coconut oil, for example, so replacing it with sweet almond oil may work as an effective substitute. Experimenting with various carrier oils can help establish what works best for you. Some popular carrier oil varieties include:

- ***For a light to medium consistency:*** Sweet almond oil, apricot kernel oil, grapeseed oil, jojoba oil, sunflower oil, argan oil

- ***For a medium to heavy consistency:*** Avocado oil, coconut oil (virgin), olive oil, hazelnut oil, macadamia oil, rosehip oil, sesame oil

Alternatively, you can also use thicker plant based butters, such as cocoa butter (fluffy consistency) or shea butter (a slightly sticky and solid mass before warming or mixing with other ingredients) depending on the texture you desire.

Be sure to store carrier oils and butters in a cool, dark place to extend their shelf life. Carrier oils should have a light, nutty aroma—if the oil has a strong, bitter aroma it may have gone rancid.

Keeping your Pores Clog-Free

Many oils contain wonderful benefits for our skin, but when using oil (or any ingredient) on our skin you have to consider whether it is comedogenic, meaning, likely to clog pores. If you are prone to comedogenic reactions (i.e. bumpiness on the skin, acne or irritation after applying certain oils), it's important to familiarize yourself with various ingredients to understand the relationship your skin has with it.

Some heavier oils such as olive oil, for example, may clog pores for those with sensitive or acne-prone skin and are better used as a wash or scrub to minimize clogging effects. Whereas jojoba oil and argan oil tend to work well with most skin-types and can even alleviate acne. These reactions can vary from person to person—what may work fine for some people might pose as an issue for others. There are no definite results so you will need to make a personalized decision and evaluate which oils work best with your skin type. Whichever oils you choose, always look for organic and 100% pure with no added nasties.

Keep in mind that some of the ingredients in these recipes are interchangeable. You can make alterations to accommodate to your skin type, to suit your personal preferences or to utilize what you have on hand.

CHAPTER 1

A Natural Approach to Radiant Skin

Effective Exfoliants, Scrubs and Masks with Kitchen Ingredients

Taking care of your skin has never been this easy. We'll use the healthy foods found right in your kitchen to make cleansing and restorative skin care products. From nutritive avocados to stimulating coffee grounds, you'll learn to take the simplest of ingredients and design your own exfoliants, scrubs and masks for cleansing, nourishing and hydrating your skin.

Nourishing Oat and Almond Exfoliant

The ingredients in this recipe have anti-inflammatory and antioxidant properties offering a soothing and hydrating treatment for all skin types. An excellent exfoliant for gently cleansing pores. Appropriate for body care as well as facial exfoliating.

Ingredients:
- 1 Tablespoon ground oats *(choose gluten-free oats if you are gluten intolerant—this ensures you will avoid any possible systemic reaction from cross-contamination)*

- 1 Tablespoon ground almonds
- ½ teaspoon rice flour
- 2 teaspoons warm water *(or oil of your choice)*

Directions:

Combine and mix ingredients, and wait until oats have slightly softened. Gently rub onto your skin in a circular motion for 1-2 minutes, avoiding the eye area. Leave on for 10 minutes and then rinse with warm water. Follow with a cold rinse.

Tip:
Adding 2 cups of oats to your bath is effective in soothing and healing various skin conditions including dry, itchy skin.

Refreshing Lemon and Apple Exfoliant

Excellent for oily skin, lemon juice has alpha-hydroxy acids which enhance dead skin cell removal. As an exfoliant, lemon will help cleanse and refresh your skin. This recipe is specifically formulated for facial skin use.

Ingredients:

- 1/8 cup lemon juice *(for sensitive skin, pure aloe vera juice may be used instead)*
- ¼ cup apple juice
- ¼ cup water
- ¼ cup cane sugar *(or jojoba beads for a gentler exfoliant)*

Directions:

Mix all ingredients in a glass jar or bowl until sugar is dissolved. Apply to skin with a cotton ball or clean, soft washcloth. Gently massaging in and rinse after 10 minutes with warm water.

Tip:

Dab diluted lemon juice to the skin (and rinse with cold water after 5 minutes) to reduce skin discoloration and fade acne scarring.

Exhilarating Vanilla Coffee Scrub

Energize your skin with the antioxidant and anti-inflammatory properties of coffee. This scrub tones and firms your skin and can help reduce the appearance of cellulite. Though created to be used on any part of your body, this compound is gentle enough for your face.

Ingredients:

- 3 Tablespoons coffee grounds *(can be from your freshly brewed pot!)*
- 1 Tablespoon sugar *(or jojoba beads for a gentler exfoliant)*
- 2 Tablespoons almond oil *(or other oil of your choice)*
- ¼ teaspoon of vanilla extract

Directions:

Mix ingredients together and massage into desired skin area. Leave on for 10 minutes and rinse with warm water. Pat dry. This can be stored in the refrigerator for a few months.

Tip:

You can use cotton pads to soak up any leftover, cooled, brewed coffee and place under your eyes for 20 minutes to help reduce dark circles and puffiness.

Restorative Lavender Sugar Scrub

A soothing scrub suitable for all skin types (particularly dry or sensitive skin), this treatment also makes for a luxurious and relaxing bedtime routine.

Ingredients:

- ¼ cup sugar *(or jojoba beads for a gentler exfoliant)*
- ½ cup coconut oil *(or other oil of your choice)*
- 2-3 sprigs of dried lavender
- 4 drops of lavender pure essential oil

Directions:

Separate dried lavender buds from sprigs. Place buds and other ingredients into a glass jar or bowl and mix. Rub a small amount onto desired area, especially effective for hands and feet. Let it set for 5 minutes before rinsing off with warm water and patting dry. This recipe stores well for several months in the refrigerator.

Maple Tangerine Peel Treatment

Rich in antioxidants and vitamins A and C, this tangerine-based mask brings about silky skin and a refreshed feel. Works well on dry patches or irritated skin.

Ingredients:

- 2 tablespoons ground and dried tangerine peel *(peel can be dried in oven at lowest heat for an hour or on tray for a few days on the counter)*
- 1 teaspoon ground flax seed
- 1 teaspoon maple syrup
- 1 teaspoon water
- 1 teaspoon coconut oil *(almond oil will also work nicely)*

Directions:

Mix all ingredients together, gently apply to desired skin area (also safe for facial application) and leave on for 10 minutes. Rinse with warm water and pat dry.

Tip:

Consuming ground flax seeds with their high content of vitamin E and omega-3 fatty acids nourishes hair follicles and lessens hair loss.

Softening Avocado Facial Mask

For nourishing and hydrating dry skin, it's hard to beat nutrient-packed avocados. Its natural oils include vitamin E oil which leaves your skin feeling silky smooth. In combination with vitamin A rich carrots, this formula acts as an excellent antiseptic as well.

Ingredients:

- ½ ripe avocado mashed
- 2 Tablespoons cooked, mashed and cooled carrot
- 1 Tablespoon olive oil *(more oil may be added for dryer skin)*
- A few drops of lemon juice

Directions:

Mix all ingredients together and rub onto face in circular motions. Leave on for 15 minutes. Follow with a warm water rinse, then a cool rinse and pat dry.

Tip:

Carrots with their high content of antioxidants provides anti-aging benefits. A mashed carrot mask may also be used on its own.

Turmeric Banana Sunshine Mask

This powerful anti-aging facial remedy is packed with antioxidants, vitamins and minerals, and will leave the skin feeling firm and radiant. Turmeric contains antibacterial, antifungal and anti-inflammatory properties making for an effective acne treatment. This recipe is suitable for all skin types.

Ingredients:

- 1 small banana
- 1 teaspoon of powdered turmeric
- 1 Tablespoon coconut cream *(or plain coconut yoghurt)*

Directions:

Place banana into a bowl and mash well with a fork. Add coconut cream and turmeric powder. Mix until smooth. Apply mixture onto face and leave for up to 20 minutes. Rinse with warm water and pat dry. Take caution not to stain your clothes or towels!

Tip:

Turmeric may be added to your natural shampoo products to reduce dandruff and to inhibit hair loss.

Sweet Cinnamon Lip Scrub

Using brown sugar and spicy cinnamon, this homemade formula is a delicious way to exfoliate dry skin and plump up your pout.

Ingredients:

- ¼ cup brown sugar
- 1 Tablespoon almond oil
- 1 teaspoon cinnamon powder

Directions:

Mix together all ingredients and apply to your lips. Scrub gently in circular motions with your fingertips and leave on for 5-10 minutes. Rinse with warm water and follow with an oil based lip balm. This may be stored in the refrigerator for several weeks.

Tip:

Cinnamon inhibits bacterial growth and makes an excellent preservative for your homemade body care products.

These luscious exfoliants, scrubs and masks are made to be an integral part of a total body care system, created by you with the purest of ingredients. They are most effective when followed by a rich and nourishing body butter, balm or lotion. The next chapter will empower you to design your own.

CHAPTER 2

Softening and Beautifying Your Skin

Luxurious Body Butters, Balms and Lotions

For radiantly soft skin it's important to keep your skin moisturized. The following recipes will help you do just that with nourishing, natural ingredients. Aloe, with its high content of vitamins and anti-inflammatory properties, is soothing to the skin, whilst coconut oil acts as a deep lasting moisturizer and strengthens and tones your skin too. Add in luxurious butters, organic oils and aromatic essential oils to achieve spa-worthy products of your own design.

Tropical Coconut Body Butter

This body butter makes an excellent hydrating treatment for all skin types with a heavenly vanilla twist.

Ingredients:

- ½ cup almond oil
- ¼ cup coconut oil
- 1/8 cup candelilla wax
- 1 teaspoon vitamin E oil
- 5 drops of vanilla essential oil *(or 1 teaspoon of vanilla extract)*

Directions:

Combine all ingredients in a glass jar, put lid on, and place jar in a medium saucepan filled with 1-2 inches of water. Turn heat on low and allow ingredients to melt. Mix all ingredients thoroughly and let cool, with jar uncapped. Apply as you would a body lotion. Shelf life is about 4 months at room temperature.

Tip:
Coconut oil makes a perfect natural shave cream.

Revitalizing Peppermint Body Butter

Enjoy the refreshing feel of this invigorating body butter. Both peppermint and grapeseed oil help regulate your skin's natural oil production, making this formula excellent for oily skin.

Ingredients:
- ½ cup coconut oil
- ½ cup cocoa butter
- ½ cup shea butter
- ½ cup grapeseed oil
- 10-20 drops of peppermint pure essential oil

Directions:

Melt coconut oil, cocoa butter and shea butter on lowest heat on the stove. Once melted, remove from heat, mix well and allow to cool a bit around 10 minutes before adding grapeseed oil and peppermint essential oil. Mix again and chill for about an hour in the refrigerator. Once it has begun solidifying, it is ready to be whipped with a hand mixer until it has a light, whipped consistency. If you live in a warmer climate and find the butter has melted, simply re-chill and whip. This body butter lasts up to 6 months at room temperature.

Tip:

Grapeseed oil makes an effective carrier oil in skin products for those with acne.

Moisturizing Shea Butter Lip Balm

Your lips will love the glossy feel of this moisturizing lip recipe. This balm works wonders for chapped and sun or wind-burned lips.

Ingredients:

- 3 teaspoons coconut oil
- 1/2 teaspoon candelilla wax
- 1 teaspoon shea butter
- 6 drops of peppermint pure essential oil

Directions:

Melt the coconut oil, wax and shea butter at lowest heat on your stovetop. Once melted, remove from heat, and cool slightly for ten minutes before stirring the in essential oil. Pour into container of your choice and let cool for about 30 minutes. You can use your own recycled balm containers or you can purchase eco-friendly paperboard or plastic tubes online.

Tip:
Candelilla wax, derived from a Mexican desert shrub, makes an excellent vegan alternative to beeswax.

♥

Sensual Cocoa Vanilla Lotion

You will truly be pampering yourself with this all-natural vanilla scented creation. The cocoa butter works wonderfully in restoring and soothing irritated or dry skin on the body and face.

Ingredients:

- 1 cup cocoa butter
- ½ cup coconut oil *(for oily skin, apricot kernel oil may be used)*
- ½ cup almond oil
- 1 Tablespoon vanilla extract *(or ground vanilla bean)*

Directions:

Melt the cocoa butter and coconut oil on low heat on the stove. Stir in almond oil and vanilla. Cool in the refrigerator for about 20 minutes until it starts to solidify. Use electric mixer or food processor to whip until mixture has a buttery consistency. You can store extra mixture in a glass jar at room temperature for longer shelf life of up to 6 months.

Tip:

A small amount of vanilla extract in olive oil makes a quick remedy for kitchen burns.

Nourishing Orange and Aloe Body Lotion

This super hydrating formula will ensure your dry skin is moisturized and toned. Its fresh orange scent will leave you feeling invigorated. This lotion is enriching for all skin types.

Ingredients:

- ½ cup almond oil
- ¼ cup cocoa butter
- ¼ cup aloe vera juice *(more if you prefer a thinner consistency)*
- 20 drops orange pure essential oil

Directions:

Melt almond oil and cocoa butter together over low heat in a saucepan. Remove from heat and blend mixture while adding the aloe juice very slowly. Continue blending then allow to cool for ten minutes before adding essential oil. Blend again until the texture is smooth and even. Pour into jar of your choice and use liberally. Shelf life is about a month, so smaller batches may be desirable.

Tip:
Aloe vera has both wound healing and pain relieing properties making it especially effective on burns, bites and stings.

Sweet Jasmine Hand Lotion

This lotion is formulated to hydrate and condition dry, rough hands, leaving them silky soft and nourished.

Ingredients:

- 1/8 cup shea butter
- 1/8 cup cocoa butter
- ¼ cup avocado oil
- ¼ cup pure aloe vera gel
- 10 drops jasmine pure essential oil
- 5 drops grapefruit pure essential oil *(or other citrus, such as orange, tangerine or lemon)*

Directions:

Melt shea butter, cocoa butter and avocado oil together over a low heat in a saucepan. Remove from heat and slowly blend in aloe vera gel. Mix well to create a milky consistency and allow to cool for at least ten minutes before mixing in the essential oil. Blend again thoroughly and pour into a jar of your choice. Let cool completely and apply as needed. Shelf life is about a month, so smaller batches may be desirable.

Tip:

Having an aromatic bath with 8-10 drops of jasmine essential oil is known to promote confidence and relieve stress.

Natural Sunscreen Lotion

This effective sunscreen lotion is formulated to protect your skin from harmful rays without the use of synthetic ingredients. For extra protection, reapply every few hours and after swimming or perspiring.

Ingredients:

- ¼ cup shea butter
- 2 Tablespoons non-nano zinc oxide powder *(ensure not to inhale powder)*
- ¼ cup coconut oil
- 1/8 cup candelilla wax
- 20 drops carrot seed oil
- 1 teaspoon vitamin E oil
- 5 drops tea tree oil

Directions:

Combine shea butter, coconut oil and candelilla wax in a glass jar, put lid on, and place jar in a medium saucepan filled with 1-2 inches of water. Turn heat on low and allow ingredients to melt. Remove from heat and let cool for a few minutes. Add non-nano zinc oxide powder (taking caution not to inhale it), and stir mixture well to distribute all ingredients. Place in the refrigerator until texture thickens and rebottle as desired. The shelf life of remaining mixture is up to a few months. This lotion has an SPF of approximately 15+. You can add more non-nano zinc oxide for higher SPF protection.

Tip:
Add a couple of Tablespoons of non-nano zinc oxide to another one of your favorite lotions for added sun protection.

Once you start making your own natural body butters and lotions you may never want to go back to commercial brands. The nutrient packed ingredients will provide you not only with moisturizing benefits, but will soothe and protect as well. You've begun a lifetime of beautiful skin with your own creations. Be sure to see more ways to pamper your body in my next chapter about bath products.

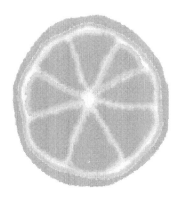

CHAPTER 3

Indulge Your Body with Natural Bath Products

Making Your Own Bath Salts, Soaps, Steam Inhalations and Massage Oils

Having a daily cleansing routine that includes aromatic baths, inhalations and massage is probably one of the best and most enjoyable ways to take care of your skin and relieve stress at the same time.

Rejuvenating Rosemary Bath Salts

Boost your mental clarity and prepare yourself for the day with a refreshing bath made from rosemary. The sulfates in the Epsom salts act as a strong detoxifier leaving your skin feeling refreshed.

Ingredients:

- 1 cup Epsom salts
- ½ cup sea salt
- ½ cup baking soda
- ½ cup ground oats *(choose gluten-free if you are sensitive)*
- 2 Tablespoons of dried rosemary or a few chopped sprigs of fresh

- 20 drops of rosemary essential oil
- ½ cup of dried rose petals *(optional)*

Directions:

Mix all ingredients together and store in a glass jar. Shake gently before using and measure about 1 cup into your bath once a week. Excess mixture will keep for a few months at room temperature.

Tip:

For easier clean up, put bath salts in a large tea infuser or doubled up piece of cheesecloth tied, letting the hot bath water run over it as you draw your bath.

Luxurious Lavender Bath Crystals

Lavender disinfects as it relaxes the mind, all the while enhancing your circulation. A must have for the faithful bather.

Ingredients:

- ½ cup Epsom salts
- ½ cup sea salt
- ½ cup baking soda
- ½ cup of dried lavender flowers
- 2 Tablespoons slippery elm powder
- 1 capful of cranberry juice extract
- 20 drops of lavender essential oil

Directions:

Mix all ingredients in a large bowl. Stir well and add more cranberry juice extract until you have a nice purplish tint. Put in about ½ cup of mixture into your bath as the water runs. Stores well in a glass jar for a few months.

Tip:

Slippery elm is one of nature's most powerful emollients for softening all skin types. A few teaspoons of just slippery elm will work well in a soothing bath.

DIY Fizzy Bath Bomb

This homemade fizzy bath bomb recipe is a fun way to relax and pamper your body with nourishing salts and oils. These also make for great DIY gifts that your friends and family will love!

Ingredients:

- ½ cup Epsom salts *(or sea salt)*
- 1 cup baking soda
- ½ cup citric acid *(from your health store or online)*
- 2 Tablespoons coconut oil
- 3 teaspoons witch hazel *(or water)*
- 5-10 drops of your preferred essential oil
- A few drops of all-natural food coloring *(optional)*

Directions:

Combine all dry ingredients in a bowl and mix well. In a separate bowl, mix together coconut oil, witch hazel, essential oil and food coloring. Slowly add wet ingredients to the dry ingredients while stirring quickly until color is even throughout. It is normal for the mixture to foam slightly. Once properly combined, mixture should hold together when pressed in your hands without crumbling (you can add a dash more liquid if it's too dry). Firmly press mixture into a greased or silicon mold of choice (i.e. heart-shaped muffin tin or ice-cube tray) and allow to dry overnight. Once completely dry, remove from mold and store in an airtight jar or container.

Tip:
Using beet juice or beet powder in replacement of food coloring also gives a nice tint.

Grapefruit Hand and Body Liquid Soap

This recipe, perfect to leave by your bathroom or kitchen sink, makes a gentle cleanser and rejuvenator for oily skin. The uplifting scent and disinfecting properties of grapefruit essential oil create a fresh foaming soap.

Ingredients:
- Pure liquid Castile soap
- Water
- ½ teaspoon olive oil
- 40 drops of grapefruit essential oil

Directions:

Using a recycled, washed hand soap pump container or shampoo bottle, fill to within 1 inch of the top with water. Then add 2 Tablespoons of Castile liquid soap and add in olive oil and drops of essential oil. Shake gently before each use.

Tip:
For extra sensitive skin, try chamomile essential oil instead of grapefruit.

Coconut Vanilla Milk Bath

Treat yourself to a luxurious, cruelty-free, Cleopatra-like coconut milk bath, which will leave your skin hydrated and silky smooth. Epsom salts contain magnesium which can be absorbed through the skin while soaking, relieving muscle aches, stress, and tension headaches.

Ingredients:
- 2 cups coconut milk powder *(or non-dairy milk powder of your choice)*
- ¼ cup Epsom salt
- ½ cup sea salt
- ¼ cup baking soda
- 10 drops of vanilla essential oil *(or scent of your choice)*

Directions:

Add all ingredients to bath while the water runs. Relax and enjoy your soothing milk bath for at least 20 minutes.

Tip:
Add ½ cup Epsom salts to your foot soak to help soften rough skin and soothe sore feet.

Luscious Lemon Massage Oil

Using this zesty massage oil is not only relaxing; it improves circulation and tones and purifies the skin. Lemon essential oil is especially beneficial for those with oily skin.

Ingredients:
- 1 cup almond oil
- 30 drops of lemon pure essential oil

Directions:

Place almond oil and lemon essential oil in a glass jar (a recycled tamari bottle works well) and shake lightly before using. Gently massage the skin towards the heart, except on joints, with circular motions. You can store at room temperature the remaining mixture for up to 6 months.

Cinnamon Mandarin Massaging Ointment

Feel the luxury and vigor that cinnamon and mandarin essential oils add to this celestial massage formula. This massaging ointment recipe is suitable for all skin types.

Ingredients:

- 1 cup grapeseed oil
- 25 drops of mandarin pure essential oil
- 25 drops of cinnamon pure essential oil

Directions:

Mix ingredients in a glass jar. Massage as needed.

Tip:

Add a few tablespoons of this formula to your bath for extra warming and stress relief.

Restorative Pine Needle Foot Bath

Try this refreshing and deodorizing foot treatment with its wonderful antibacterial and soothing benefits.

Ingredients:

- ½ cup chopped fresh pine needles
- 2 cups boiling water
- ½ cup Epsom salts
- 15 drops of eucalyptus pure essential oil
- 5 drops of pine pure essential oil

Directions:

Make a pine needle infusion by pouring 2 cups of boiling water over pine needles into a heat resistant bowl or pan. Cover and steep for at least 30 minutes. Add in other ingredients and pour it all into a large pot or bucket filled halfway with water as hot as you can stand. Soak your feet for 10-15 minutes. Add cool water if too hot.

Tip:

You can drink some of the pine needle tea while you soak your tired feet, giving a nice vitamin C boost.

Relaxing Aromatherapy Bath Oil

Roman Chamomile Pure Essential Oil will transform your bath into a therapeutic treatment, acting as a sedative, a pain reliever and an antidepressant. This recipe is excellent for sensitive skin.

Ingredients:

- ½ cup oil of your choice *(almond or olive oil work well)*

- 20 drops of roman chamomile pure essential oil
- 10 drops of lavender pure essential oil

Directions:

Mix all ingredients and add to bath while the water is running.

Tip:

A few drops of roman chamomile in any oil can be applied to a rash for gentle relief.

Invigorating Steam Inhalations

Perhaps the simplest way to get a spa-like treatment at home, steam inhalations cleanse and detoxify your skin while offering relaxing moist heat therapy.

Ingredients:

- 1 quart (or 1 liter) of boiling water
- 5 drops of lavender pure essential oil
- 1-2 drops of tea tree oil

Directions:

Remove boiling water from heat and pour carefully into a large Pyrex or other heat safe bowl you have placed on the table. Sit down and hold a large towel over you and the bowl. Let the steam treat your face for 10 minutes. Finish with a cool rinse.

Tip:

Tea tree oil makes an effective wart treatment when applied in a tablespoon of oil to affected areas twice a day for 2-3 weeks. Dilute in more oil if you have sensitive skin.

Once you've cleansed and relaxed your body and soul with your homemade bath products, you can prepare fresh organic elements for restoring damaged hair, skin and nails with the recipes in the next chapter.

CHAPTER 4

*Nutritive DIY Formulas for Nails,
Hair and Skin Restoration*

All Natural Treatments, Balms and Hair Products

In today's busy world we sometimes have to allow a little time to take extra care of our bodies. Using these gentle, non-toxic formulas that you make at home, with ingredients like coconut milk and avocados, you can be sure that your skin is receiving the best care possible.

Simple Vitamin E Nail Treatment

This simple yet effective treatment will strengthen your nails and stimulate growth.

Ingredients:
- A few drops vitamin E oil *(capsules broken open or in bulk)*
- A few drops olive oil *(optional)*

Directions:
Mix vitamin E and olive oil together in a small bowl. Dip fingers into the oil mixture and massage gently onto each nail before going to bed. Wipe any excess oil

off with a washcloth. Repeat every night for 2 weeks to nourish dry, brittle nails.

Tip:

Vitamin E oil also soothes sunburns when applied topically.

Deep Conditioning Avocado Hair Mask

This recipe will hydrate your hair leaving it super soft and shiny, and works wonders for use on dry hair.

Ingredients:

- ½ mashed avocado
- 1 Tablespoon olive oil
- 1 Tablespoon coconut oil
- 1 Tablespoon agave nectar
- ¼ cup water

Directions:

Mix all ingredients together and comb into wet hair, making sure to apply evenly from roots to ends. Towel up and leave on for 10 minutes. Follow with a cool rinse.

Tip:

For oily hair simply replace avocado with 1 cup of strawberries blended with the other ingredients.

Easy to Make Rosemary Shampoo

Bring mental focus to your morning with a rosemary scented shampoo, which stimulates hair growth and treats a dry scalp. This recipe is great for all hair types.

Ingredients:

- ½ cup pure Castile liquid soap
- ½ cup water
- 16 drops rosemary pure essential oil
- 2 drops peppermint pure essential oil

Directions:

In a clean, recycled shampoo bottle, add all ingredients and shake gently. Use a few squirts, massaging onto your scalp and hair.

Tip:

This formula also makes a refreshing body wash.

Natural Shine Hair Conditioner

This formula, using maple syrup and coconut milk, is great for all hair types, particularly long or thick hair. It works to add shine, detangle and nourish the scalp.

Ingredients:

- 1 cup coconut milk
- ¼ cup maple syrup
- 2 Tablespoons almond oil

Directions:

Mix all ingredients and pour into a recycled shampoo or conditioner bottle. After shampooing and rinsing hair, apply this conditioner liberally and massage into your hair from roots to ends. This is a perishable product and will last a few days at room temperature or a week or two in the refrigerator.

Tip:

Plain coconut milk can be added to your bath for silky smooth skin.

Balancing Herb and Vinegar Rinse

To restore your pH balance and remove residue build-up in your hair, try this interchangeable herbal recipe.

Ingredients:

- ¼ cup apple cider vinegar
- 2 cups herbal infusion (*to make an infusion bring 2 cups water to a boil, remove from heat and pour over herbs. Steep for 15-20 minutes and let cool*)

Herbs to use:

For dark hair - **parsley**

To darken graying hair - **sage**

For bringing out highlights in lighter-colored hair -
chamomile

Directions:

Choose the herb of choice according to your hair color.
After the infusion has cooled, add it to the apple cider
vinegar. After shampooing, massage about a ½ cup or
more of the mixture into your hair, being sure to apply
it from the roots to the ends. May be rinsed with warm
water followed by a cool rinse, or simply left on. The
smell of vinegar will disappear once your hair is dry.
Recommended as a once per week treatment.

Tip:

**Apple cider vinegar by itself makes a great
wash for acne. If you have sensitive skin, be
sure to perform a patch test first.**

Homemade Hairspray

Add some oomph to your hair without breathing toxic
chemicals. This alcohol-free hairspray will both style
and nourish your hair at the same time.

Ingredients:

- 1 cup hot water
- ¼ cup pure aloe vera juice

- 2 Tablespoons sugar
- ½ teaspoon vitamin E oil
- 10-15 drops of your favorite citrus pure essential oil *(lemon, orange, grapefruit or tangerine)*

Directions:

Boil water in a small saucepan and add sugar and stir until dissolved. Allow mixture to cool and add aloe vera juice, vitamin E oil and essential oils. Pour mixture into a fine mist spray bottle and shake well.

Tip:

When consumed, aloe vera juice can help promote hair growth with its rich vitamin and mineral content.

One Ingredient Make-Up Remover

This super simple and effective method works even on your most stubborn, waterproof make-up.

Ingredients:

- Coconut oil - *In some climates, where room temperature is cooler, you may want to warm the jar of coconut oil in a pan of water on low heat until you have a small amount of softened coconut oil.*

Directions:

Using a teaspoon or two of the softened coconut oil, apply to your face and eyes (keeping eyes closed when you are in that area) and massage slowly, followed by gently wiping off the makeup and oil with a cotton pad.

Tip:

Apply a bit of coconut oil to your lips before bed for a moisturizing overnight treatment.

Cooling Cucumber Face and Body Mist

Perfect for hot summer days or to simply add moisture and nutrients into your skin, this refreshing face and body mist will keep your skin feeling hydrated and fresh.

Ingredients:

- Juice of 1 cucumber *(use a juicer or alternatively you can blend and strain through a cheesecloth to extract juice)*
- ¼ cup water
- 1 teaspoon aloe vera gel
- 1 Tablespoons rosewater

Directions:

Pour all ingredients into a fine mist spray bottle and shake well. Mist onto the skin as desired. Store in refrigerator for about one week.

Tip:

To reduce puffy under eyes or dark circles, simply place chilled, sliced cucumber to closed eyes for 15 minutes. There's a reason why this old-aged cliché is still celebrated.

Restorative treatments for your skin are important in retaining that youthful glow and feel. Once you feel revived, it's time to pamper yourself with all natural make-up and body products. In my next chapter I'll teach you simple recipes to accentuate your natural beauty.

CHAPTER 5

Making a Dazzling Impression

Organic Homemade Make-Up, Body Powders, Deodorant and Toothpaste

If you ever wanted to save a little money on your makeup and body care products, here is your chance to do just that with amazing fruits, plant-based oils, vegetables and more!

Beautiful Beetroot Lip Gloss

Treat your lips to a splash of color with all natural, organic ingredients.

Ingredients:

- 1 Tablespoon almond oil *(apricot kernel oil works for this recipe, too)*
- 1 Tablespoon beetroot powder - *to make, slice a few beets very thinly and dehydrate at 100°F (38°C) for 10 hours, or until they are dry and crispy. Use a coffee grinder to create a powder. Strain through several layers of cheesecloth to get any larger particles out.*
- 1 Tablespoon shea butter

Directions:

Melt oil with shea butter on a low heat, stir in 1 Tablespoon of beetroot powder. Pour into a small container. Use more powder if a stronger color is desired, less for a lighter tint.

Tip:

Fresh beetroot or beet juice can be applied directly to the cheeks for a rosy tint.

DIY Arrowroot Foundation Powder

This foundation formula, appropriate for all skin types, is light and smooth in texture and will leave you with a silky soft feel. Gives light coverage with a matte finish.

Ingredients:

- ½ cup arrowroot powder *(add more for lighter color)*
- ¼ cup cocoa powder *(add more for darker color)*
- ¼ teaspoon powdered cinnamon
- ¼ teaspoon powdered ginger *(to add warmth for yellow undertones - a small dash of turmeric will work too, but use sparingly!)*
- 2 teaspoons bentonite clay
- 10 drops vitamin E oil
- 10 drops tangerine pure essential oil *(may use less for sensitive skin)*

Directions:

Stir dry ingredients well in a large bowl and gradually tweak ratios until the mixture closely matches your skin tone (you can test it on the back of your hand). Stir in essential oil and vitamin E oil. Store in a container or glass jar and apply with your favorite foundation brush.

Tip:

Arrowroot on its own makes the perfect baby powder or dry shampoo (just add cocoa powder for darker hair).

Pure Berry Blush Powder

Using freeze dried raspberries, this formula uses the simplest and purest ingredients to give your cheeks a healthy glow.

Ingredients:

- 1 Tablespoon freeze dried raspberry powder *(or you can powder whole freeze dried raspberries in a coffee grinder)*
- ¼ teaspoon arrowroot powder *(more for lighter color, less for darker)*

Directions:

Mix ingredients together until you achieve your desired tint. To deepen the color you may also add a dash of cocoa powder or cinnamon. Store in an airtight container and brush onto the apples of your cheeks, as desired.

Homemade Liquid Eyeliner

Using plant-based materials on your eyes just makes sense. This recipe allows for beautifully defined eyes without any harmful ingredients.

Ingredients:

- 1 teaspoon coconut oil
- 1 ½ teaspoons pure aloe vera gel
- ½ teaspoon cocoa powder *(for a brown hue)* or 1-2 capsules activated charcoal *(for a black hue)*

Directions:

Mix ingredients well and store in a small airtight container. Apply with your favorite eyeliner brush.

Tip:

Using spirulina powder in replacement of the cocoa powder/activated charcoal will give a deep green color.

Homemade Defining Mascara

Using activated charcoal and gentle ingredients that won't irritate your eyes, this formula helps bring out those luscious lashes naturally.

Ingredients:

- 2 teaspoons coconut oil
- 4 teaspoons pure aloe vera gel
- ¼ teaspoon grated carnauba wax *(you may want to add more if you want the mascara to be a little more waterproof)*
- ¼ teaspoon bentonite clay
- 1-2 capsules activated charcoal

Directions:

Warm coconut oil and carnauba wax on low heat until melted. Remove from heat and stir in aloe vera gel, bentonite clay and ½ teaspoon activated charcoal (after carefully opening the capsules—this can get messy). To squeeze into a new mascara dispenser, pour the mixture, once cooled a bit, into a small freezer bag. Squeeze the mixture into one corner of the bag and make a tiny cut on the opposite corner. Insert the cut corner well inside the mascara tube and squeeze the mixture out, very carefully and slowly. Alternatively, you can simply place the mixture into a small container and dip in your mascara wand as needed. Keep lid on tight to keep moisture in.

Tip:

Believe it or not, a sprinkle of activated charcoal on your toothbrush once or twice a month will whiten your teeth! Again, take care not to get the powder on clothing.

Arrowroot Talc-Free Body Powder

A dusting of this arrowroot and herb powder will freshen your body naturally without any toxic ingredients.

Ingredients:

- 1 cup arrowroot powder
- 1 cup white clay powder
- 1 Tablespoon comfrey powder
- 1 Tablespoon slippery elm powder
- 25 drops lavender pure essential oil

Directions:

Stir all ingredients in a large bowl, thoroughly and store in a glass jar. A glass salt-shaker works well for a sprinkle effect.

Tip:

Comfrey powder added to your bath helps with wound healing and acts as a pain reducer.

Gently Effective Shea Butter Deodorant

Smell great and feel fresh with this all-natural deodorant balm.

Ingredients:

- 3 Tablespoons coconut oil
- 3 Tablespoons baking soda
- 2 Tablespoons shea butter
- 2 tablespoons arrowroot powder
- 10 drops bergamot pure essential oil

Directions:

Slowly melt the coconut oil with the shea butter on low heat. Add in baking soda and arrowroot and mix well. Let cool for at least ten minutes before adding essential oil. Pour directly into cleaned and recycled deodorant dispenser and allow to solidify. Keep in cool storage, especially in warmer climates.

Tip:

A drop of bergamot essential oil in a teaspoon of grapeseed oil (olive or almond oil would also work) gives an effective treatment for cold sores.

Sweet Rose Deodorant Spray

Containing soothing ingredients, this mist is an effective yet gentle deodorant with antibacterial properties, suitable for sensitive skin.

Ingredients:

- ¼ cup pure aloe vera gel *(or aloe vera juice)*
- ½ cup witch hazel
- 2 teaspoons mineral salts *(Himalayan salt or sea salt work well)*
- 10 drops rose geranium essential oil *(or essential oil combination of your choice)*

Directions:

Place all ingredients into a spray bottle with a splash of warm water and shake well until salts have dissolved. Spray a few times under each arm or on feet. Let dry for a few seconds or gently pat dry.

Tip:

Aloe vera gel mixed with witch hazel makes for soothing sunburn relief. Witch hazel has been used for centuries by Native Americans as a medical astringent, providing relief for inflammation, irritation and itching.

Blossom and Pink Grapefruit Perfume

For a sweet floral scent that will captivate, this homemade perfume is just right for you. You can experiment with measurements and other essential oils to create your own signature scent.

Ingredients:

- 6 drops pink grapefruit pure essential oil
- 5 drops of rose geranium pure essential oil
- 1 drop ylang ylang pure essential oil
- 1 cup water

Directions:

Mix all ingredients and store in a small spray bottle or mister. Take care not to spray in your eyes, and try a little at a time.

Tip:

Ylang ylang essential oil is a natural sedative and aphrodisiac and makes a romantic addition to your massage oils.

All Natural Whitening Toothpaste

This formula works for giving you that sparkling, healthy smile and fresh minty breath.

Ingredients:

- 6 teaspoons baking soda
- ¼ teaspoon hydrogen peroxide *(3% solution or less)*
- 2 Tablespoons coconut oil, warmed to liquid
- 5 drops spearmint pure essential oil

Directions:

Combine and mix ingredients, adding more baking soda if mixture is too runny, less if too dry. Store in an opaque container in a cool place.

Tip:
Disinfect your toothbrush with hydrogen peroxide to keep germs astray.

Refreshing Minty Mouthwash

This antibacterial mouthwash will leave your mouth feeling clean and minty fresh.

Ingredients:

- ½ cup pure aloe vera juice
- ½ cup water
- 5 drops peppermint pure essential oil
- 5 drops spearmint pure essential oil
- ¼ cup hydrogen peroxide *(3% solution or less)*
- 1 teaspoon sea salt
- ¼ teaspoon liquid stevia *(optional for a touch of sweetness)*

Directions:

Place all ingredients in a dark or opaque container and shake well. Shake mixture before each use and gargle and swish around mouth for a couple of minutes. Rinse mouth afterwards and do not swallow mouthwash. Will store for two weeks in a cool, dark place out of sunlight.

Tip:

Hydrogen peroxide, when diluted in equal amounts of water, can also be used as a quick mouthwash to neutralize canker sores (but not to be ingested).

The recipes you've just read will help you look your best with cruelty-free, all natural beauty products. Read on to learn easy ways to give extra love to your face.

CHAPTER 6

Therapeutic Facial Care

Cleansers, Toners and Intensive Treatments for that Beautiful Face

In this chapter, using simple ingredients like witch hazel, rose petals and green tea, will help you create a multitude of ways to give your face, whatever your skin type, the special care it needs.

Gentle Chamomile Facial Cleanser

This gentle formula will cleanse and penetrate the skin whilst leaving it hydrated and satiny soft. Suitable for all skin types, particularly dry or sensitive skin.

Ingredients:
- ½ cup pure Castile liquid soap
- ½ cup chamomile tea, cooled
- 1 teaspoon avocado oil
- 10 drops lavender pure essential oil

Directions:
Mix all ingredients in a lidded jar or container of choice and shake gently before use. Lightly splash face with water and massage cleanser onto face in circular motions before rinsing.

Tip:

Avocado oil applied as a facial mask helps soften lines and wrinkles.

Oil Cleansing Method

The simplest of ingredients can be the best for your skin. The oil cleansing method may seem daunting to those with oily skin, but it can moisturize, remove impurities, dissolve sebum (without stripping your skin) and even clear up acne whilst leaving your skin with a radiant glow. It may take some experimenting and adjusting to achieve the perfect oil cleansing combination for your skin type.

Ingredients:

- One or more of the following astringent oils: *Castor oil, sweet almond oil or hazelnut oil*
- One or more of the following conditioning oils: *Apricot kernel oil, argan oil, rosehip oil, jojoba oil, avocado oil, sunflower oil or grapeseed oil*

Choose oils depending on your personal preference and what works best for your skin. A combination of any of these oils can be used to make up the desired ratio—you may choose to use 3 oils, for example.

Ratios:

- For oily skin, use: 30% astringent oil to 70% conditioning oil

- For dry skin, use: 10% astringent oil and 90% conditioning oil
- For combination skin, use: 20% astringent oil and 80% conditioning oil

Directions:

Begin by mixing together your chosen oil combination ahead of time. Soak a washcloth in hot water (but at a comfortable temperature for your skin) and place hot washcloth over your face for 30 seconds to open the pores. Remove cloth and apply the oil cleansing mixture on to your face by gently massaging in circular motions for two minutes. Let the oils sit in the skin for an extra 30 seconds. Rinse face and use washcloth to gently wipe and remove any excess oil. Rinse washcloth and repeat step until all oil is completely removed.

Tip:
Adding a couple drops of tea tree essential oil to your mixture acts as a natural antiseptic to prevent breakouts.

Revitalizing Rosewater Toner

This freshening toner works for all skin types as it nourishes your skin and minimizes the appearance of pores.

Ingredients:

- 1 cup rosewater
- ½ cup witch hazel

Directions:

To make your own rosewater, simmer 2½ cups of water with 2 cups of rose petals until liquid is reduced by ½ (about 30 minutes). Let cool and strain. Place ingredients into a spray bottle and shake well. Lightly spritz onto the face after cleansing.

Tip:

This same recipe can be used as a refreshing setting spray. Spray lightly over your makeup and air dry for a dewy finish.

Anti-Aging Aloe and Jojoba Oil Facial Serum

This formula will keep your skin fresh and soft using anti-aging ingredients like non-greasy jojoba oil. Perfect for all skin types including oily skin.

Ingredients:

- ½ cup pure aloe vera gel
- 3 teaspoons almond oil
- ½ teaspoon carnauba wax
- 3 Tablespoons jojoba oil
- 10 drops chamomile pure essential oil

Directions:

Melt carnauba wax with almond oil on low heat. Mix well and let it cool for at least 15 minutes. Add aloe and chamomile essential oil, and then mix again. Apply a handful or two to your face after removing make-up or as a freshening morning ritual, followed by a cold splash. Store in airtight container.

Tip:
Because of the non-greasy and anti-inflammatory nature of jojoba oil, it also makes a soothing treatment for acne.

Tea Tree and Green Tea Acne Relief Mist

This easy-to-make and fresh smelling mist provides a soothing sensation, especially therapeutic for oily skin or acne due to its antibacterial properties.

Ingredients:
- 1 cup green tea, cooled
- 3 drops tea tree pure essential oil

Directions:

Pour tea and the essential oil into a fine mist spray bottle and shake gently. Shake before each use and close eyes whilst misting onto the face.

Tip:

Boiled green tea poured into a large heat-proof bowl with some dried peppermint leaves provides a therapeutic steam inhalation. Simply put a large towel over your head and the bowl for 10 minutes.

Firming Aloe Eye Gel

A refreshing anti-wrinkle eye gel that helps firm the under-eye area and fight fine lines.

Ingredients:

- 2 teaspoons pure aloe vera gel
- ½ teaspoon vitamin E oil
- ½ teaspoon witch hazel

Directions:

Place ingredients into a small airtight container and mix well. Gently dab gel on the delicate skin around the eyes, at night or when desired.

Tip:

Apply pure vitamin E oil to the skin to fade the appearance of scars or stretch marks.

Miracle Night Cream Mask

This nourishing overnight treatment is perfect for sensitive skin and all skin types. Using gentle and non-greasy apricot kernel oil, you will wake to start your day with soft, supple skin.

Ingredients:

- ¼ teaspoon carnauba wax
- 1 teaspoon coconut oil
- 2 Tablespoons apricot kernel oil

Directions:

owly melt wax with oils on a low heat, and let mixture cool at room temperature. Massage gently onto face before bedtime.

Tip:
Pure apricot kernel oil makes a captivating and aromatic massage oil on its own.

THANK YOU

You may have reached the end of this book, but your journey to organic skin and body care has just begun. Not only will you reap natural beauty, but also a healthier you—and let's not forget that you are helping our furry friends, too.

After trying these natural recipes and feeling the benefits, I hope you are inspired to continue making healthier everyday choices, not only for your body, but for the planet as well.

Thank you so much for sharing this journey with me. I hope that this book will become your lifelong guide to creating your own organic and all natural skin and body care products.

A WORD FROM THE PUBLISHER

Hi, I'm Carmen, a holistic health geek with a passion for health, herbalism, natural remedies, as well as whole-food and plant-based lifestyles. After resolving various health issues I have struggled with for many years, I aim to inspire and help improve your health and longevity by sharing the tireless hours of research and valuable information I have discovered throughout my journey. Through the power of nutrition and lifestyle, with an evidence-based approach, I believe you can achieve your health and wellness goals.

If you enjoyed this book, I would love to hear how it has benefited you and invite you to leave a short review on Amazon - your valuable feed-back is always appreciated!

*You are invited to to join our **Free Book Club** mailing list. Sign up via our website to receive **special offers** and **free for a limited time** Health & Wellness eBooks!*

'A conscious approach to health & wellness'

carmabooks.com

72349929R00045

Made in the USA
Middletown, DE
04 May 2018